Stop, Wait, Go!

Road Signs and Symbols It's Fun to Know!

by Nancy King

King, Nancy
Stop, Wait, Go!
/ Nancy King.
ISBN-13: 978-1539542148

Published by King Design, Inc., East Windsor, New Jersey, USA
NancyKingDesign@gmail.com

First Edition
First Printing: January, 2018

Printed in the United States of America.

ISBN-13: 978-1539542148
ISBN-10: 1539542149

Stop, Wait, Go!

Road Signs and Symbols It's Fun to Know!

by Nancy King

*T*his is a book about road signs and symbols. A symbol can be a picture or a letter.

*S*ymbols tell you a message without words.

*S*ymbols are important because they can tell you what to do, or where to go, and they can help to keep you safe.

*S*igns and symbols are everywhere. In this book you will see what many road signs and symbols look like, and what they mean.

Mr. and Mrs. Lee, Alan, and Emily are going on a road trip. They will drive on Highway 66.

2.

They are packing lunch for all of them into their car, but where will they eat?

Let's go along and find out.

This sign tells people not to walk on their lawn.

This sign says children may be crossing the street on their way to school.

ELEMENTARY SCHOOL

4.

Oh, it's starting to rain! This sign warns drivers that the road may be slippery when wet.

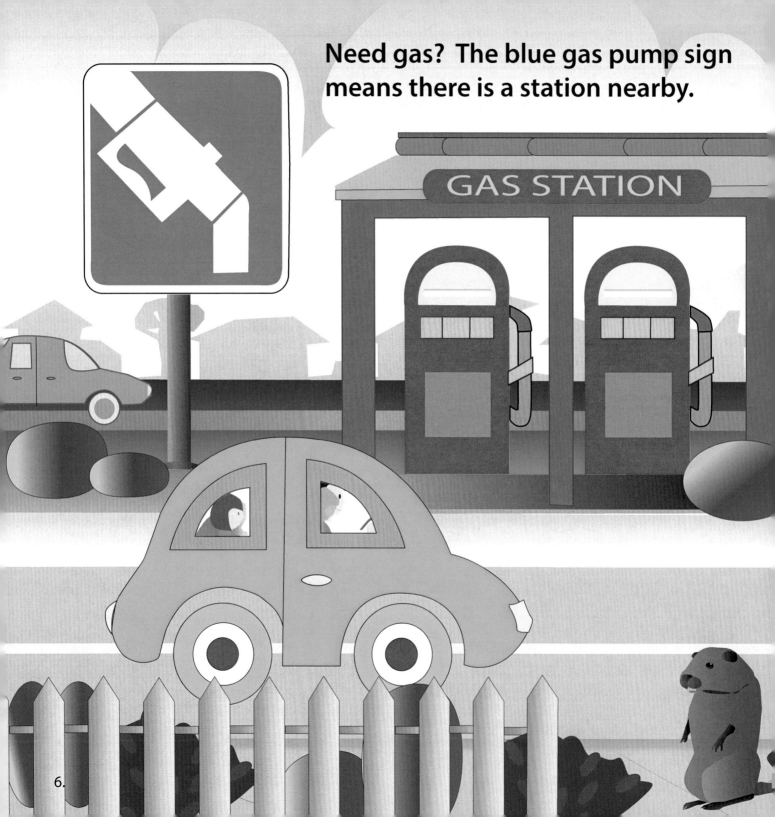

Need gas? The blue gas pump sign means there is a station nearby.

This sign shows that places to eat, park a trailer, find a Wi-Fi outlet or a room to sleep, are nearby.

Emily asks, "Are we there yet?"

This sign is telling traffic to stop, to protect the workers in the road. The traffic will stop until it is safe to drive again.

The two "R" letters and the big "X" stand for Rail Road Crossing. This sign shows where trains will be crossing the road.

9

This symbol warns drivers to be on the lookout for deer crossing the road.

Bicycle riders know they are allowed to ride their bicycles where they see this sign.

The man and lady symbols say there is a bathroom nearby.

The wheelchair symbol says it can be used by people in wheelchairs.

Rest Rooms

On the way, Alan notices a road sign showing a swimmer in the water.

It means that there is a place nearby where swimming is allowed.

The Lee family is hungry and ready for lunch. Would you be hungry after a long trip in a car?

This sign points the way to picnic tables in the park.

14.

The Lee's car approaches Yosemite National Park. Hikers who see this sign know that safe walking trails are nearby.

PARK ENTRANCE

There is a special area to leave their car.
On a green sign they see a "P" for Parking,
and drive into the lot to find a space.

A red circle with a red line
across it means "No".
This sign means No Left Turn.

The Lee family sees a sign that shows a picnic table. This means they should follow the arrow to the area where they can eat.

Hooray! Mr. and Mrs. Lee have found a good picnic table.

The litter basket sign reminds them to keep the area clean.

TRASH

18.

A Smokey the Bear sign alerts people to be careful when lighting fires.

Now they can finally enjoy lunch!

How many signs

1.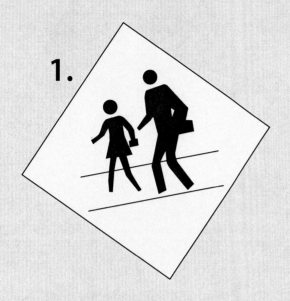

2.

3.

4.

can you remember?

See answers below.

5.

6.

7.

21.

DICTIONARY OF SYMBOLS

Warning! Danger ahead! Color and shape are very important in traffic signs. The yellow diamond shape is used as a warning sign.

SCHOOL CROSSING	HILL	SLIPPERY WHEN WET	DEER CROSSING

A red sign means Warning! or Stop!

ONE WAY - DO NOT ENTER   IN CASE OF FIRE USE STAIRS   EMERGENCY EXIT   STOP HERE

A red line across a circle means NO!

NO TRUCKS   NO RIGHT TURN   NO LEFT TURN   NO PARKING

DICTIONARY OF SYMBOLS

Blue signs are friendly. They will help you find what you need when you are on a trip.

PICNIC
AREA

ELECTRONIC
SERVICE

LITTER
BASKET

GASOLINE
STATION

BATH ROOMS

HOSPITAL

HANDICAPPED
CAN COME IN

SWIMMING
AREA

Green signs are guide signs

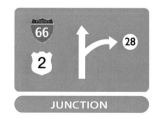

HAPPY TRAVELS!

Acknowledgment

*Many thanks to Mrs. Helen Ducoff for her helpful
contributions to the development of this book.*